# Women in Bloom

Personal Stories of Women

Who Returned to College

And Other Words of Inspiration

By Carol Mattson

Text written and edited by Carol Mattson

Cover design and photograph by Carol Mattson

© 2017

ISBN 978-1-931001-31-1

## Dedication

This book is dedicated to my wonderful sisters and mentors Velda and Sharon and to my college counselor Mary Shaw, who encouraged me and countless other women to believe in themselves!

I would also like to especially thank each and every one of the women who participated in the interviews and for their willingness to tell their stories. Although their stories are real, names have been changed to protect their identity.

# Forward

Dr. Carol Mattson's collection of stories took me back to 1970 when I too decided to return to college and the fear and uncertainty I felt in my early beginnings. I can relate to these stories and I know that Carol does too because she has also taken this journey. Her book addresses some of the typical roadblocks women who want to return to college sometimes experience such as, *I'm too old*; *I'm afraid*; *I feel guilty about time away from family and the expense of college*; and *I may not succeed.* It also speaks to a variety of needs, intrinsic to oneself, or extrinsic, to support oneself and/or children, which often propel women to seek higher education.

Upon reading Dr. Mattson's manuscript, I was struck by the enormous support these women received through counselors, women's self-esteem classes, encouraging teachers and their own strength of character. Each story has in common ones desire for personal growth and transitions, requiring on their part commitment, support and courage. The desire to take that "first baby step" and "go for it" somehow emerges deep within, which becomes more compelling than fears of failure and a variety of other excuses. Any woman, no matter her age, educational, familial or life experience backgrounds, will be inspired by Dr. Mattson's collection of personal stories, *Women in Bloom.*

**Marci Taylor Stewart, MFT**

Watercolor Artist

Author, *Flowers and Thorns; A Caregiver's Story*

# Table of Contents

## Introduction

Over many years, I had the privilege of hearing the courageous and inspiring stories of many women who returned to college. Without such inspiration, I am not sure I would have made it this far in the process of my own growth. It is for this reason that I write this book. It is my attempt to share stories of individuals who for one reason or another returned to school in search of a better future for themselves and their families. My hope is for readers to identify with at least one person who can provide them with the encouragement they need at this time in their life.

The stories are based on real life experiences. I selected and interviewed women at various stages in their educational process. Each story is a subtle reminder that personal growth is a journey and often challenging along the way. Yet on the upside of every challenge is an increase in one's self-image and accomplishments beyond our comprehension. One of the women is just starting school and a little uncertain. Others are moving uphill and a little tired. Some are close to their destination, and a few have arrived.

These women can look back and breathe a sigh of relief at what they have endured, while they share with us the rewards of their accomplishments and encourage those around them to keep on growing.

I vaguely remember that afternoon on campus when I sat in a teacher's lounge at Fullerton College with a room filled with "non-traditional aged" students, mainly women. It was a luncheon for re-entry students and coordinated each semester by Mary Shaw. Mary was the counselor I met with prior to registering for my first class. She personally invited me to the luncheon, and she encouraged me to attend.

As I sat in the room full of strangers I began feeling very sorry for myself. I felt uncomfortable and began wondering what I was doing there. Finally I found the courage to speak to a younger woman sitting next to me. I shook my head and said, "I don't know if I can do this. My husband is not real supportive, I have two young children, and money is really tight." I was probably hoping that she would help me talk myself out of this school stuff! Instead, she calmly and assertively replied, "I'm a single parent, I have three children, I work full-time, and I'm graduating in June." I couldn't believe what I was hearing. She had not given me the empathic response I was hoping for but rather had humbly challenged and encouraged me by her own example.

That day, one speaker after another stood up and shared their stories. One talked about her tremendous fear of algebra and told us how she dealt with text anxiety. Another spoke about her struggling marriage and how she recently survived a difficult divorce. One woman who needed financial assistance to continue her education learned how to get financial aid at the college to help her pay expenses. More than one shared how very helpful Mary's Self-Esteem class was as she taught them about realizing their self-worth.

Overall, they shared their trials, and most importantly, they shared their successes. They had learned there was indeed, a plan for their lives.

*For I know what*
*I have planned for you,*
*says the LORD.*
*I have plans to prosper you,*
*not to harm you.*
*I have plans*
*to give you a future*
*filled with hope* [liii]

Jeremiah 29:11

---

## *Ways to know you are a returning student...*

You think you are the only student in class who doesn't know what the professor is talking about

You can remember when John F. Kennedy was President

You wonder how some people can spend 15 hours a day in the Student Union, doing nothing

Everyone stares in disbelief when you tell them you're "just here to learn"

Your favorite shoes are older than most of your classmates

You suddenly notice one day that you are asking more questions than the rest of the class combined

You suspect that the girl next to you paid more for her jeans than you paid for your first car

You're the first one to arrive in class and the last one to leave[iii]

# Alice

*...I feel like a victim of circumstances*

Alice recently started back to school at a community college. She has worked full-time since she graduated from high school. She is single, has no children, and lives on her own.

I'm just starting college, and I want to get a degree. I'm thirty-six years old. I feel like I have wasted my whole adult life in a dead-end job. My work hasn't gotten me anywhere. I am going back to school now, but I feel like it is going to take me forever to get a degree. This has affected my attitude lately, and I feel like a victim of circumstances.

# I Can Begin Again

*Alone again in a crowded room*
*Cornered by the questions in my mind*
*It's so hard to understand*
*How a life that I had planned*
*Stole my joy and left me far behind*

*Chorus:*
*I can begin again*
*with the passion of a child*
*My heart has caught a vision of a life that's still*
*worthwhile*
*I can reach out again*
*far beyond what I have done*
*Like a dreamer who's awakened*
*to a life that's yet to come*
*For new beginnings are not just for the young*

Words by Dave Clark and Larnelle Harris

# Maria

*My parole officer knew that I wanted to go to school and work with kids. He said, "Why don't you?" He took an interest in me, and that made me want to work with the system.*

Maria completed about half of the coursework she needs to meet the requirements of an Associate of Arts degree in human services. She has one child and lives with another woman who has two children. Her educational goal is to complete a Bachelor of Arts degree in art therapy and work with at risk children.

I have been in and out of prison most of my life. By the time I was sixteen, I had a child. I was involved in drug use and hanging out with the wrong people. My attitude was poor, and my self-esteem was low. I felt that the people who were supposed to be helping me were just working for the dollar and didn't really care about me. When I was in counseling, I wasn't getting what I needed.

Right after I got out of prison for the last time, my ex-girlfriend died of AIDS. That's when I decided I needed to make some changes in my life. My parole officer knew that I wanted to go to school and work with kids. He said, "Why don't you?" He took an interest in me, and that made me want to work with the system.

I went to a community college and saw a counselor. She told me to take the placement test to determine which college courses would be appropriate for my skill level. Two of the classes that I took when I started back to school were *Drugs and Alcohol in our Society* and *Self-Esteem*. The information I received in these classes helped me understand myself and believe in myself. I haven't used drugs for over six years now.

I am currently involved in the Human Services Club on campus, and I volunteer in the *Head Start*[iv] program. I love to draw, paint and do murals. I do a lot of the art work for the Human Services Department. I want to be an art therapist. I have learned to listen and set goals, and I believe I can reach my goals. I plan to transfer to the university in the fall of next year.

# Thinking

*If you think you're beaten, you are.*
*If you think you dare not, you don't.*
*If you'd like to win, but think you can't,*
*It's almost for sure you won't.*
*If you think you're losing, you've lost...*
*For out in the world we find -*
*Success begins with a person's will,*
*It's all in the state of mind.*
*Life's battles don't always go*
*To the one with the better plan.*
*For more often than not, you will win*
*If only you think you can.*

By Walter Wintle

# Nancy

*I have the life experiences, I'm getting the education, and I'm trying to put it all together.*

Nancy is close to completing her Associate of Arts degree in social psychology. She is currently separated from her husband and has a two-year-old son who is living with her. This semester she is looking into various four-year degree programs where she can transfer and get a Bachelor of Arts degree and possibly a Masters in the social services area. Eventually she would like a career working with at risk youth.

When I started attending community college following my graduation from high school, they didn't have matriculation[v]. When I went to the campus for the first time, I felt so intimidated that I didn't want to see a counselor. I went through the whole enrollment procedure by myself. I just took classes that sounded fun or easy. My course work consisted of aerobics and skiing. It was an enjoyable experience at first, but I was just going down the road to nowhere. I had no direction, so I quit for a while.

When I was thirty-two years old, I started back to school again. This time I went through the process of meeting with a counselor. I also enrolled in EOPS[vi]. A counselor in EOPS helped me work out an academic plan and a time management plan, which helped me with my study skills. In order to participate in EOPS, qualify for book grants, and meet my financial aid requirements, I have to carry at least 12 units each semester. Every semester I go to my counselor, get on my knees, and with tears in my eyes beg her to let me go down to 9 units in order to make my load a little lighter. I've done it so often that it's become a joke, but I still beg her for permission to take a lighter load each semester.

Currently, I am separated from my husband, taking care of my two-and-a-half-year-old son, and living on AFDC[vii]. My son is on a 58-hour school week along with me. I get extended child care in the evenings through CARE[viii]. I use that time for studying my math and getting caught up on assignments that are due the next morning, but sometimes it is really hard.

The CARE program wants students to take 12 or more units and shoot for 14. I can understand them wanting me to get off AFDC and get to work, but at the same time, my family is falling apart. I honestly feel that if I were taking 6 units, I would be an excellent mother and person. At 9 units I would be a good mom and an okay person. At 12 units and above, it is affecting my motherhood, and it is affecting my life. To me, this is ironic.

I keep saying next semester I am going to go without the special programs and book grants. I promise everyone around me. Then I just add more units each semester and I get crazier. My friends say, "Gosh, I can't believe you're doing this. You look so skinny." I guess I do it because it is such a feeling of accomplishment.

I grew up in a retired military family. I don't think my parents thought any of their kids would even finish high school. Finances were so tight that college was never an option. Currently my grade point average is

4.0. Sometimes, even now, I send my grades home to my dad, and he sends me $3 back in the mail. My GPA motivates me because it will allow me the opportunity to transfer to a university.

I find that my volunteer time on campus also helps keep me motivated. My major is in the direction of social psychology, so my involvement in different clubs and activities allows me to work individually and in groups with people of various ages and cultures. I have been exposed to many differently situations that people face, and I believe this will help prepare me when I go into social work.

As a teenager, I didn't graduate with my high school class in the traditional way. I put myself through the school of hard knocks - juvenile hall and foster homes. When I was younger, I didn't want to deal with the uncomfortable part of life. I wanted to wipe it all away. Now that I'm older, I can see that certain things happen for a reason. I've learned a lot from my early experience. My field of study is psychology; and with what I have learned, now it is all coming together. I have the life experiences, I'm getting the education, and I'm trying to put it all together.

*TOUGH SEMESTERS NEVER LAST,*
*TOUGH STUDENTS DO.*

Robert H. Schuller

# Betty

*My grandson is thirteen years old. He said, "Grandma, how old are you now? Aren't you ever going to get out of school?"*

Betty will complete her Associate of Arts degree in social sciences next semester. She has been widowed for six years and has six grown children. One of her sons lives with her. She is not planning to transfer and hasn't decided what she will do following graduation.

I am kind of a piece of walking history. I was born in the depression and went through World War II and the Korean War. During World War II I was living on a farm and couldn't get to school, so before I started at the community college, I had only completed school through the eighth grade.

I started back to school after my husband passed away. My children were concerned about me sitting at home doing nothing. They asked me what I would like to do. I had always been busy as a hospital volunteer, but I decided I would like to go to school. I always wanted to go to school, and I wanted to know if I could do it. It was a personal challenge. My children gave me their support and told me to do what I wanted to do. My family is my strength. My children watch me with my studies and say, 'Now you know what we went through.'

My grandson is thirteen years old. He said, "Grandma, how old are you now? Aren't you ever going to get out of school?" I said, "Some day." I think he's wondering if he's going to have to go to school for so long. On my birthday last year I got a note from my granddaughter who said that by me going back to school at my age, I had encouraged her to go back to school. She's twenty-seven.

The first college class I took besides a class for re-entry students was English. I wanted to learn how to write a family journal for my children, since I'm the only one still living in my family who is left to tell them anything. The first day of class, the professor told us to write a short essay. I was petrified! It had been forty-some years since I had done anything like that. I wrote what I could.

At the next class meeting he put the names of students on the board that he wanted to talk to. Of course mine was up there. He kept me after class and helped me through that class and the next English class I had to complete before I could take college level English. We're still good friends, and I still go and talk to him. I don't know what I would have done if he had turned me away.

All of my teachers have been great. Now, if I have a problem or concern, I talk to them and tell them where I am coming from. One teacher actually treated me differently after I talked with her.

Although I haven't completed my journal, I have written and collected pieces for it through all of my class work. In a multicultural class, I wrote about my husband and his aunt who were Italian immigrants. His aunt sent me some very interesting information on the family.

Entering college has been quite a challenge for me. I had no high school education, and I certainly had no idea of how to do college work. It is still very hard for me. It takes all the concentration I have. Every course

I've taken has been a challenge, but I am determined that I can do it.

Each semester I take seven units: two academic classes and one exercise class. I have some physical limitations, so I take an adaptive physical education class to keep my body strong. I also get support academically and emotionally on campus through the Re-entry Center[ix] and the Learning Center[x].

Next semester I am going to take a class on marriage and parenting. It is one of the courses required to finish my Associate of Arts degree in social science. Having been married for forty-two years and having raised six children, I should be able to pass that one. If I get through all of my classes, I will graduate in the spring. Once I complete my A.A. degree, I don't know what I might do, because I didn't think I was going to go this far.

# Let Me Grow Lovely

*Let me grow lovely, growing old--*
*So many fine things do:*
*Laces, and ivory, and gold,*
*And silks need not be new;*
*And there is healing in old trees,*
*Old streets a glamour hold;*
*Why may not I, as well as these,*
*Grow lovely, growing old?*

By Karle Wilson Baker

# Eileen

*He said, 'You? You're a woman, and you don't even have a degree." I thought, nobody is ever going to say that to me again; and I went down and enrolled in school.*

Eileen has a Bachelor of Science degree in business and has recently completed a graduate certificate in career counseling.  She has been single for almost twenty years and is engaged to be married. She has no children. She would like to find a rewarding part-time position utilizing her career counseling skills.

I had never enjoyed school.  And although I wasn't an A student in high school, I managed to get B's without ever opening a book.  When I was young, all I wanted to do was work, earn a living, get married, and have babies.  By age thirty I was divorced, and I did not have any children.  I was working as a statistical clerk on a large company project and essentially doing the work for my boss, but I wasn't getting paid what he was getting paid.  So when a position became open in my department, I decided to try for a promotion. My boss said, "You? You're a woman, and you don't even have a degree."

I decided nobody is ever going to say that to me again, and I went down and enrolled in school. I went to a community college, took the entrance examination, and enrolled in sociology. My company paid my tuition; and for the next ten years, I worked forty to sixty hours per week and took classes off and on.

Once I enrolled in an accelerated program[xi] at a university where I was working on my business degree. I had an opportunity to go to Europe with one of my friends, so I decided I would take a semester off. It wasn't until two years later that I started back to school again.

I'm just not a school person. I didn't think the degree was worth it. Then I heard people say, "You're degreed or not degreed. Two or three years of college on a resume are meaningless." So I started back to another university to complete my Bachelor of Science degree in business administration. It was a grueling program, but when I was finished, I was rewarded with a good pay raise. I was the first member of my family to earn a college degree. My mom was thrilled!

Seven years later I was laid off, after eighteen years with the same aerospace firm. I didn't know what I was going to do. My company provided career guidance through an outplacement[xii] service. I was so impressed with my career counseling that I decided to pursue a fifteen unit graduate certificate in career counseling at a local university.

It had been seven years since I had completed my BS degree, and now I was starting work toward a graduate degree. I was scared! It was different going into a Master's program. I had no confidence in writing papers. I was wondering if, at age forty-eight, I could still learn like I used to. I was also concerned as to whether I had the necessary study skills.

In every class I took, I told everybody in the class that I was scared. All of my classmates and my instructors were very supportive. They encouraged me a great deal and helped build my confidence.

*No matter what you say or do to me,*
*I am still a worthwhile person*

Author Unknown

# Margaret

*Although my first year of college was severely stressful, I somehow managed to graduate four years later with a 3.97 grade point average, earning a Bachelor of Science in elementary education and human development with a minor in art.*

Margaret earned a Bachelor of Science degree in elementary education and human development with a minor in art at a public university. She has three grown children and is married to her second husband after the death of her first husband. Margaret is a published author and professional artist.

As a young woman about to graduate high school, I wanted to be an artist and live in Greenwich Village in New York City. When my parents nixed that plan, I landed in nurse's training. In addition to art, my number one desire was to be a wife and mother. Two years into the program I married my husband, a recent Naval Academy graduate who had opted for a career in the Marine Corps, in a military wedding. After a brief honeymoon, we drove across country to his first duty station.

As my husband prepared for his departure to Vietnam, our family was under severe stress. I often wondered if our marriage would survive his year-long deployment or possible death during the hell of war. At the time I was employed as a kindergarten aide but sensed that I wanted to be a "full-fledged teacher," and that required a bachelor's degree and elementary education credential. I met other marine wives in my husband's company who all had college degrees and felt envious and regretted my decision at eighteen to be an artist. So before my husband left, he offered to help me figure out the requirements listed in the university's catalog, and I decided to go to college to get that degree.

Since I was an over-achiever, I signed up for 19 hours, against my husband's advice. The entire time, I was terrified about my decision. Still, the entire process of enrolling only pushed me forward. After the first week of classes, I dropped Economics 101, stayed with 16 hours, and prayed for at least a "C" in each class.

When grades were posted at the end of the first semester, I had straight A's. Then I heard a negative voice from within scream, "You don't deserve these grades and didn't do A work!" In spite of looking and sounding like a competent, confident 33-year old woman, inside my demons convinced me to question the grades. I went to each professor and argued against the A. Each one assured me I had done outstanding work and the grade would stand.

During my husband's year in Vietnam, our three children and I never heard from him. A psychiatrist told me that when some men go into a warzone with unresolved tensions, they experience something know as compartmentalization[xiii] in order to deal with the imminent danger at hand and put aside the issues left at home. I responded by throwing myself into my studies, caring for our teenager and two younger children, running the church Sunday School, coaching a basketball team, and serving as Girl Scout cookie chairwoman. When I was at college, wonderful friends and neighbors helped with my kids. Somehow, despite my busy schedule, I managed to grab any free, unallocated minute to study and write papers.

The toll my husband's year long silence levelled on each one of us was heartbreaking. By the grace of God, he returned in one piece and we gradually reassembled the broken pieces of our marriage and family. Although my first year of college was severely stressful, somehow I managed to graduate four years later with a 3.97 grade point average earning a Bachelor of Science in elementary education and human development with a minor in art.

*You never know how strong you are until being strong is the only choice you have.*

Author Unknown

# Diane

*The speaker at the seminar said, "If you have nothing to invest, invest in yourself." That is when I decided to start back to school.*

Diane recently completed her coursework for a Master of Arts degree in counseling. She received her Associate in Arts degree in liberal studies from a community college and a Bachelor of Fine Arts degree in communications from a private university. She has been married twenty-three years and has two daughters, ages nine and sixteen. She has two part-time positions and is currently looking for a full-time position.

My husband and I were going through some very difficult times financially. I had gone to a financial planning seminar to see if there was something I could do to improve our situation. The speaker at the seminar that day said, "If you have nothing to invest, invest in yourself." That is when I decided to start back to school.

It wasn't the first time I had decided to go back to school. I dropped out of high school and got married. I finally received my high school diploma through an adult education independent study program at a local community college. A few years later, I decided to go back to that same college and enroll in a class or two.

By that time I was a mother of a little girl. I felt very responsible to her and very guilty for wanting time for myself. I decided that I would take two classes, one day a week, but I did not feel that I needed to talk with an academic advisor. So I enrolled in a drawing class and a sculpture class. There was one problem. I thought that college class schedule, which listed the classes as being offered on Tuesday and Thursday, meant that I could pick one of those two days.

The entire semester, I was going to school one day a week and missing half of my classes. Toward the end of the semester, one of my professors began calling students up to the front of the class to discuss with them their progress and their grades. Then he asked if there was anyone whose name he had not called. I raised my hand and he told me to come and see him. I gave him my name and when he checked his records he said, "You missed half of the classes. I dropped you from this class several weeks ago." I explained that I thought I was only supposed to be there one day a week and told him that I had completed all of the class assignments. He checked and sure enough, there were grades listed for all of the class projects. Anyway, after that I was so humiliated I did not go back to college again for almost eight years.

When I started back to college for the second time, I was fortunate that a person in the financial aid department recommended I make an appointment with a counselor who specialized in working with re-entry women. At our first meeting, this counselor told me to take the placement test before I registered for any classes. I assured her that I just wanted to take one or two classes and that I didn't really need to take a placement test. She sweetly insisted, and so I did.

I didn't' know what I wanted to do or what class I wanted to take, so I declared business as my major. After all, I was there to help "save" my husband's family business. I was also there to learn some skills in case I had to go to work. I decided that speech would be a good class to start with, just in case I had to talk myself into a good-paying job.

My counselor recommended a speech teacher. Not only did I lose the name she gave me, but I also had to petition to get into my first class because I had failed to register at the time of my appointment.

On the first day of school, I walked into a speech class with my add slip. I sat down and waited to see if the teacher was accepting petitioners. After waiting almost fifteen minutes for her to finish giving a very lengthy introduction to her class, she announced that her class was full and she would not accept any petitioners. I quickly glanced at the class schedule and found another speech class offered at the same time, but it was located in the next building. I told another student who was there petitioning, and together we ran to the other building, found the classroom, and asked the teacher if we could add his class. He smiled and signed our add slips.

That day I started back to college again. The second teacher turned out to be the one that had been recommended to me in the first place. It turned out to be a great class and a great experience. This was just one of many times that cause me to believe that nothing less than divine intervention got me through school.

The next three years were quite challenging. My husband, who was in business with his father, found out that his father had gotten behind paying taxes. As a partner of the business, my husband was also responsible for the debt. As my self-esteem was increasing with all that I was learning, my husband's ego seemed to be crashing along with his business. It was a hard time for us, both emotionally and financially. I continued taking classes, and every semester I tried to arrange my schedule around the needs of my family.

One day at school I ran into someone I had known since the third grade. She was also taking classes, and she invited me to go to the cafeteria for a soda where she was meeting two other friends. This was very out of character for me, because I was in school to go to class, not to socialize. That day, however, I agreed to take a short break with her.

She introduced me to her friends, including someone who was twenty years my senior but very cute and quite charming. He was taking a photography class and asked me if he could take my picture some time. I didn't take him very seriously and prudishly looked at him as if I didn't want to be bothered.

The next week he brought his portfolio to show me. He assured me that the picture he requested was simply to add to his portfolio and showed me some of the pictures he had taken of other students on campus. With his pleasantness and persistence, I finally agreed, with the stipulation that we remain on campus. I had done some modeling and I thought, why not?

During the next two years we remained very good friends. We spent a lot of time together on campus. In addition to studying at school and worrying at home, I started to laugh and have fun! At one time I told him I thought he was an angel that had been sent down to test me. He laughed and said, "I've never been called an angel before."

For the first time in my life, I knew what it was like to feel like a woman. I had gone from being a teenage girl to being a wife and a mother. My life at home was very stressful and sometimes very lonely. At age thirty-one, I felt old. However, being the pragmatic person that I am, I knew the grass wasn't necessarily greener somewhere else. It took a lot of work and a lot of prayer to keep our friendship a friendship and to keep my marriage and my family together.

The following summer, my mom was diagnosed with cancer. She died six weeks later. The next year my stepmother died unexpectedly of a heart attack. I had to drop a class to assist with funeral arrangements. Then I had to place my dad, who had had a stroke, in a board-and-care facility. That same year I graduated from community college with honors. With all of the stress and tragedy, the success felt extra good!

In the fall, I transferred to a small private college as a communications major. The college did not have the support system for re-entry students that I'd grown accustomed to at the community college, and the student body there seemed very young to me, very traditional.

My first week on campus I had three different students say things to me like, "Are you a student?''; ''I thought you were the teacher''; "Oh, you're a student?" It was no longer easy to schedule my classes around my family's needs as I had before. Many of the required classes were only offered every other semester, and it was important to take them when I could. I decided to talk with the director of academic support about starting a support group on campus for older students. With her encouragement, I formed a group and held meetings off and on for about a year and a half. My involvement in this project introduced me to many adult students as well as faculty and staff on campus.

In two years, I was able to finish my Bachelor of Fine Arts degree in communications by attending summer school and intersession classes. I graduated Magna Cum Laude with Department honors. I was thrilled!

After graduation, I found that the job market was tight, especially in the field of communications. As a mom, I wasn't willing to work evenings and weekends to compete with younger graduates for entry-level jobs.

I started looking for work and found a part-time job at a community college where I assisted adults with disabilities in preparing resumes and looking for employment. I loved my job, and my boss and others encouraged me to pursue graduate school.

The private college where I graduated had a Master of Arts degree program in their educational department with an emphasis in career counseling. I enrolled in the program and continued to work part-time. Recently I was offered another part-time position as a career advisor with a local school district. And, I just learned that I passed my comprehensive examination, which means that I have officially completed my Master of Arts degree, with honors!

*In making an investment decision,*
*the important factor is not what it costs.*
*You do not care what it costs,*
*But you are truly concerned with what it pays.*

Venita Van Caspel, CFP

# Wanda

*I think one of the things that got me through was my philosophy that I would never drop a class.*

Wanda has a Bachelor of Arts degree in liberal studies and recently completed her Master of Arts degree in education with an emphasis in reading. She has been married for almost thirty-five years and has three grown daughters. Currently she has a full-time tenured position teaching high school English.

I always wanted a college education, but when I got out of high school I just figured I could not afford to go to college because I came from a poor family. I got married right away, and soon thereafter I went to college for two years. I remember my first day on the campus I was enthralled at how different college was than high school. I remember loving it and thinking how glad I was to be there.

After two years, I had an associate's degree in business. I could type real well, and I thought that I wanted to be a secretary for the rest of my life, at least until I had children, because in my family, the women didn't work. They stayed home and took care of the house and the kids.

After several years of working as a secretary I began to realize that I wanted that four year degree. Also, I think one of the things that sent me back to school was when my sister divorced and I realized that nothing is certain. I wanted to be able to support myself.

I lived in a small town, and the nearest four year college was approximately a hundred miles round trip. By this time I had three daughters to take care of, and I wasn't willing to drive such a long distance to the university. When the local community college offered advanced degree classes, I took a class here and there until my middle daughter got out of high school.

I wanted to major in business, but the only degree I could get in my hometown was a liberal studies degree. I guess I just ran into the right person who said, "You know, if you get a liberal studies degree and pass the National Teacher's Examination in business, you can still do your student teaching in business;" so that is what I did. After I passed the NTE in business, my first job was teaching high school English, and that is where I have been ever since.

After I started teaching, I got into a Master's program by accident. I signed up for a class teaching reading because I thought it would be interesting and useful. I went to the first two classes and liked it, so I stayed. I figured as long as I stayed in education, the more education I received the more money I would make, and if I was going to get more education, I might as well get a Master's degree in education. I just completed my thesis on Reading and Writing Workshop with At-Risk High School Students and will receive my MA in June.

For the most part, I completed my education by going to school one night a week and taking two classes a night - one from 4 – 7 p.m. and the other from 7 –10 p.m. I found I wasn't any more tired at 10 o'clock than I was at 7 o'clock, and basically I was already tired at 4 p.m. when I got there. Going one night a week seemed to make it a little bit easier on me and my family, especially since I was working during the day.

When I look back, I know that one of the things that got me through school was my philosophy that I would never drop a class. Many of my classes would start out with an enrollment of fifty and end up with twelve students. I decided early on that I would not drop a class, and I didn't. There is a lot of personal satisfaction in having the education that I have always wanted, and I like what I am doing.

## *Don't Quit*

*When things go wrong as they sometimes will,*
*When the road you're trudging seems all up hill.*
*When the funds are low and the debts are high,*
*And you want to smile, but you have to sigh,*
*When care is pressing you down a bit,*
*Rest, if you must – but don't you quit.*
*Life is queer with its twists and turns,*
*As every one of us sometimes learns,*
*And many a failure turns about*
*When he might have won had he stuck it out;*
*Don't give up, though the pace seems slow –*
*You might succeed with another blow.*
*Often the goal is nearer than*
*It seems to the faint and faltering man,*
*Often the struggler has given up*
*When he might have captured the victor's cup*
*And he learned too late, when the*
*Night slipped down,*
*How close he was to the golden brow.*
*Success is failure turned inside out –*
*The silver tint of the clouds of doubt –*
*And you never can tell how close you are,*
*It may be near when it seems afar;*
*So stick to the fight when you're hardest hit –*
*It's when things seem worst that you mustn't quit.*

Author Unknown

# Sally

*Now I know that all things are possible when we try and trust God.*

Sally has a Master of Arts degree in Rehabilitation Counseling. She has been married for about five years to her second husband and has two daughters who are married with children of their own. She just recently retired from a position at an elementary school teaching special needs children.

I had a part-time job at the bank that seemed to be wreaking havoc with my family life. My husband at the time was working long hours and spent the weekends on the golf course. I thought if quit my job I could get everything back on track. The reality was that my marriage was coming to an end. I would soon have no husband and no job.

One day when I went to pay the daycare bill the director told me, "Sally, if you are not working or in school, you cannot keep the girls in daycare". My mind raced looking for a solution. I signed up for an accounting and business administration class at the local community college. I knew I needed the low cost daycare if I was going to go to work and take care of the girls. For a while I worked a part-time job as a bank teller, and then I found a full time job in Department of Social Services (DPSS) that paid better. Juggling the responsibilities of home, kids, work, and school seemed to get harder and harder. Then my dad died.

I was in the middle of a divorce when my dad died. It was during the summer, and I sat by the pool reading an article in McCall's magazine titled, "What Will You Be Doing Five Years from Now?" At age thirty-five, I decided I wanted to be a counselor. I thought a master's degree in rehabilitation counseling would allow me to do something that was both helpful to others and good economically.

At the time my three daughters were ages 7, 9 and 12. I had a Bachelor's Degree in Sociology that was 12 years old, and I had never worked a full time job until after my divorce at the age of 35. When I shared what I was planning with the first man I dated after my divorce, he told me, "You'll never get a master's degree one class at a time."

I thought to myself, "I'll never know until I try." I started with one class and planned out my schedule to complete my master's degree within two years. I took a leave of absence from DPSS for one year so I could go to school full-time. My schedule was altered when my oldest daughter needed back surgery and spent three weeks in the hospital. On occasion people would ask me how much longer I had before I completed my degree. I told them I didn't know, but I always let them know that God would help me get through, even though I had my doubts at times. My two years stretched to three, but I eventually received my Master of Arts degree in Rehabilitation Counseling. Now I know that all things are possible when we try and trust God.

*Trust in the LORD with all your heart and do not rely on your own understanding. Acknowledge him in all your ways and he will make your paths straight.*

Proverbs 3:5-6[xiv]

# Rhonda

*I realized at some point I was going to be divorced and I had better figure out a way I could support myself and my children.*

Rhonda has a Bachelor of Arts degree and a Master of Arts degree in psychology. She has a California state license for marriage, family and child counseling (MFCC). She is single and has two grown children who live on their own. She currently works full-time as a community college counselor, teaches part-time at a private university, and has a private practice for marriage, family and child counseling.

When I was in high school, I was a good student and very goal oriented. I knew what I wanted to do with my life. I planned to go to college and become a biology teacher. Then right after I graduated from high school, I met my future husband. All I wanted to do at that point was get married, and so I did.

I started to college, but I told myself it's going to be five years before I am done with school. That's way too long, and besides, I want to get married and start a family. I can't do it. I talked my boyfriend into getting married, and I quit college after attending one semester.

One day when I was chasing one of my children around the house, it suddenly hit me. The five years that seemed like forever when I was eighteen had gone very quickly. I realized I had not done anything with my life except have two babies. That is when I started back to school.

I began by taking art and other classes that I liked. I continued taking one or two classes a semester, and I did that off and on for about ten years. I was also raising kids, doing the Brownie mother, the Boy Scouts, the Cub Scouts, the room mother, and anything else I could do to get out of the house.

When I was twenty-nine years old, my husband relocated to Orange County, California, where he had taken a new job. While he was working and living in Orange County, I was living up north with our kids until we could sell our house. With my husband out of the house, I felt such incredible freedom. After the house was sold, the kids and I moved to Orange County too, but my husband and I had a really hard time learning to live together again.

I started taking classes again here and there. It became more and more evident to me that I was not cut out to be a housewife. I wanted to work, and I wanted to go to school. My husband did not want me to do those things. He wanted me to be a support system for him, and he resented anything that took me away from that role. That is when I realized at some point I was going to be divorced and I had better figure out a way to support myself and my children.

I decided I would go back to school purposefully, and I began taking general education classes. That was also the year I got divorced. I was very unhappy, and I decided that I could no longer stay for the sake of the financial support. During the summer, while taking two classes, I sold my house. I had to move on the day of finals, and the place I was moving into was not going to be ready. I stayed with a friend for three days. It was a real mess!

I remember the day I moved into my new place and connected the clothes dryer by myself. That was one of those points in my life when I knew it was going to be all right; I was going to survive. From then on, it was just a matter of doing it.

The following semester I took a career class because I felt I needed more focus and direction. Both art and psychology came up as high areas of interest. I decided I would have a better chance of supporting myself and my children with psychology than with art, plus I could not stand the thought of being mediocre at anything, and I was afraid I was not good enough in art.

At one point along the way, I was talking to my counselor and told her I wanted to go into psychology. She said that the program was impacted, but there was always room for people who were good, so what I needed to do was go about making myself good.

I gathered as much experience as I could and did as much as I could. I started working as a tutor on campus in the Learning Disabilities Center. I worked registration, testing, and anything else I could do part-time that fit into my schedule. I got to know people, and the people I worked with gave me tremendous support emotionally. One day my boss told me, "One thing I really like about you is when you say, "Can we do this?" and you say, "Sure we can," and then you go and do it. I don't ever have an argument, and if a decision needs to be made, I know that you'll take care of it and do a good job.

I remember when I had to go to the California State University to get a concurrent enrollment form signed. I was driving my huge old station wagon, which wasn't running very well at the time. It was raining that day, and I was scared to death the car wasn't going to make it. To top it off, I had bronchitis. I finally got there and trudged across the campus in the rain. I met the man who had to sign the form. He looked at me and said, "Well, are you just another one of those bored housewives that wants to do psychology?" I was so annoyed and answered, "No, I am not! I want a career in psychology." He signed the paper, and I transferred to the university the following semester.

Once I completed my Bachelor's program, I went in to talk to the head of the department about going into their Master's program. I graduated with honors and worked hard to complete the program within a three-year period by taking classes during intersession and summer. The man looked at my transcript and said, "Why are you bothering with our program? Why don't you go directly to the University of California, Los Angeles, and get your Ph.D.?" This was the same man who had made such a derogatory remark just three years earlier. I knew he had no recollection of what he had said to me back then, but I appreciated the validation he gave me that day.

After graduation I was tired of going to school and needed to earn some money, so I decided to put off graduate school. I remember the day I tried to get the courage to tell my mother that I was going to apply for a full-time position at the college and take a year off from school. I am her only child, and she is very ambitious for me. I was sitting on my bed talking to her on the phone. She said, "Oh, you're just going to do what you did before. You'll probably drop out, meet some man and get married again. You'll never go back to school if you don't keep going."

I hung up and sat in the middle of my bed crying. I said to myself, "For God sakes, look at you. You're thirty-eight years old, and you've made a decision for yourself. You've looked at the pros and cons and you know you can go back to school when you want to go back. You've done it before. There is no reason why you can't, and you're sitting here crying because your mother doesn't approve." That was another point of gaining my independence. I gave up needing her approval and quit school for one year.

The next year my mentor and boss who took an interest in me and said she wanted me to write and teach a career class for disabled students. In order to qualify for this project, I had to quickly apply for a temporary credential and enroll in a Master's program.

I have since completed my Master of Arts degree in psychology and have a California state license in marriage, family and child counseling. I work full-time as a community college counselor, spending two days a week doing crisis intervention in the health center and three days a week doing fine arts academic counseling. I coordinate our mental health services and supervise one intern each semester. In addition, I have a private practice and teach two career counseling classes at a

private university.  Next semester I am going to teach a
new stress management class.

# Success

*To laugh often and much*
*To win the respect of intelligent people*
*and the affection of children*
*To earn the appreciation of honest critics*
*and endure the betrayal of false friends*
*To appreciate beauty, to find the best in others*
*To leave the world a bit better, whether by a healthy*
*child, a garden patch or a redeemed social condition*
*To know even one life has breathed easier because you*
*have lived.*
*This is to have succeeded.*

By Ralph Waldo Emerson

# Ann

*She said, 'I'm really sorry, but I can only give you a B. I thought I had died and gone to heaven. I was so thrilled to think that I could do B work in a university program.*

Ann is single and has two grown children. She has a Master of Arts degree in education with an emphasis in English as a second language. Currently she is working as a professional staff coordinator at a community college and also teaches English as a Second Language.

I grew up in North Carolina. Both of my parents had a college education, so it was assumed that I would go to school and become a nurse or a teacher. I chose teacher because I did not like blood. I went to a small church-affiliated school for four years and graduated with a teaching credential. I taught high school English for a year and a half.

I ended up marrying my high school sweetheart and moving to California. He is now and was at that time a musician, so for eleven years I lived a subculture existence. I grew up in a very east coast, established, mainstream family, so for a long time it was fun living that lifestyle. After we had children it became harder, and we ended up divorcing. My children were five and eight years old at the time.

After being single for three years and working at various jobs, I enrolled in a *Careers for Women* class at a community college. I was frightened out of my mind to go back to school because my undergraduate experience had not been very pleasant academically. I was a very mediocre student with no study skills. I made mostly C's, and I graduated thinking I was stupid.

I started going to a community college using my student loans and working on campus. I was also getting a little bit of child support each month, and after I quit my job, my ex-father-in-law and my mother decided they would help me by giving me a little bit of money each month.

One of the jobs I had on campus was working in the career center. There was a computer program called *SIGI,* and it helped me realize what I wanted to do - - dress casually every day, have a group of friends around me, and get paid $100,000 a year – wasn't probable. After having lived in a subculture for all those years, I had completely lost my frame of reference for what the dominant culture was like.

I also realized that I already had training as an English teacher. One day when I was tutoring another student, she found out that I had a teaching credential. She said, "Why don't you become an ESL teacher?" I didn't know what an ESL teacher was, so she explained it to me and arranged for me to have coffee with one of her former teachers who taught ESL. This teacher told me they were getting ready to start a certificate program at a local university. This sounded intriguing to me, because I loved culture studies and I was already an English teacher.

After further investigation, I tiptoed into my first university class frightened out of my mind again. The world of ESL had a whole language in itself. I did not know what they were talking about. When I went to the teacher for a final interview at the end of the class to turn in a project, she said, "I'm really sorry, but I can only give you a B." I thought I had died and gone to heaven. I was so thrilled to think that I could do B work in a university program.

September was approaching, and my children would be going back to school. I was home with no income, no school, and no excuse to beg, borrow or steal. One of my friends was terminally ill with cancer. I was turning forty years old. My boyfriend of almost six years was moving away, and I was a real mess. I was probably the most depressed I have ever been in my life.

I went to a community college and interviewed with a woman who ran the refugee project to talk about working with her as an ESL teacher. She told me that I did not want to be an ESL teacher because it was not stable and that I should probably look for something else. When I left there that day, I cried all the way home. I decided to write her a letter. I thanked her for her time and told her I would still like to be an ESL teacher. She interviewed me in September and offered me a job in November. The job was a temporary position for one year. I was making $16.20 an hour. I was able to work and go to school and complete the certificate program.

It took me five years to complete the certificate program, and then I realized that if I wanted a contract position with a college, a Master's degree would be required. So I worked two jobs and went to school a couple of nights a week to complete my MA degree. I eventually got hired back at the community college, where I worked seven years as the coordinator of the ESL and Adult Basic Education program for continuing education.

Now I work as a professional staff coordinator, as well as teach classes. At the end of each semester when I give my students their certificates, I wear my cap and gown. I tell them going to school was a struggle for me, but I never gave up.

In order to keep going, there were a lot of support systems I put myself into. I remember feeling terribly embarrassed about where I was and why I was there and comparing myself to my friends who had stayed on track. One thing I did was join a women's support group that I found through a private counselor. The women in the group were all in places where their lives were changing and they needed to grow. It was great to meet others and network with women who were in a similar situation. That group continued for three years.

*As important as your past is,*
*It is not as important as the way you see*
*your future.*

Tony Campolo

## What is Holding Us Back?

### FEAR

Fear can range all the way from uneasiness to panic. Although it is natural to be anxious about doing something difficult, fear can cause us to talk ourselves out of doing what needs to be done.

### ECONOMICS

In many instances we rely on economic assistance from our spouse, significant other or parents. While economic assistance can first appear to be a blessing, it may become a curse. If we find it difficult to invest in ourselves, we may one day suffer the consequences of a subsidized life.

### DESIRE TO PLEASE

If our feelings of self-worth come from pleasing others, we become confused about what we want. This can sometimes have tragic consequences. When we work towards meeting our own basic needs, we are more free to please others.

### FEELING GUILTY

If we are in the habit of disregarding our own needs because we have been accused of being selfish, then we may feel guilty when we stand up for what we want. Or we may feel guilty because our needs seem to be in conflict with our family's needs. Guilt may blind us and prevent our doing what we need to do.

## COMFORT

Many times we do not challenge ourselves to grow or make changes when there is no compelling need. When things are calm, we don't want to rock the boat, even though we know it is best to be prepared for the storm.

## PROCRASTINATION

Through procrastination we avoid the issue. We tell ourselves that there will be a better time, but there is never a good time to do what we find difficult. When a decision is put off once or twice, it becomes increasingly easier to keep putting it off. Soon we do not even think about doing it. We just worry because we have not done it.

## What To Do

Set a realistic, practical goal. Meet with an academic advisor or career counselor. Take some assessment tests to determine your personality, aptitudes, interests and values. Choose classes and begin by taking only the number of units you believe that you can successfully complete during a semester. Keep in mind your personal lifestyle and other responsibilities including family, job, etc.

Plan concretely, logically and realistically how you are going to reach your goal. A.) See a financial aid officer. B.) Meet with an academic advisor. C.) Study the catalog and decide what courses you need. D.) Become familiar with student support services and get affiliated with those that can best meet your needs.

Get your plan well in mind and program yourself for calmness. Anticipate the kinds of reactions you might receive and how you will respond to them. You may get sidetracked if you have not anticipated road blocks.

When you make a commitment to your educational plan, be calm, logical and confident. Do not apologize for what you are doing or try too hard to get friends and family to understand. Understanding is desirable, but it is not essential. Some may never understand, so do not let this hinder you.

Do not present the plan to others as though you are asking for approval. When we seem uncertain, others may become anxious. If your plan is well thought out, there is less chance anyone will object.

Get started, stay focused, and don't quit. If you find you need to slow down or change direction, that's okay. Be supportive of your efforts and don't be too hard on yourself.

## What Might Happen

You might be surprised to find out that others accept and approve of what you want to accomplish.

You may also find that others are trying to talk you into changing your mind through ambiguous statements or comments that incite guilt or doubt such as, "I don't think you understand"; or "What about the children"; or "If you want to do something, why don't you just get a job". These are attempts to manipulate or sidetrack you. Don't get trapped in the confusion. You won't win by arguing. Stay focused.

Of course when one or more persons in a relationship change, the relationship also changes. During this time it's important to be true to yourself. A relationship that depends on servitude is unhealthy.

## You WILL Bloom and Grow!

# About the Author

Dr. Carol Mattson holds a Doctorate in Educational Leadership and a Master of Arts Degree in Counseling. She is an author, teacher, counselor, speaker, group facilitator and innovator.

She loves to encourage people, particularly women, to search for and find an appropriate and rewarding plan for their lives.

# End Notes

ii Scripture and/or notes quoted by permission. Quotations designated (NET) are from the NET Bible® copyright ©1996-2006 by Biblical Studies Press, L.L.C. All rights reserved.

iii Inspired by a handout given by Professor William Womack. Adapted from an article by Dale E. Reich, published in the Chronicle, April 14, 1982, Vol. 24, No. 7

iv Head Start is a children's education program for preschoolers who live with families living below the poverty level.

v Matriculation: an agreement between the college and its students to ensure academic success. It includes 1) assessment 2) orientation 3) counseling/advisement and 4) student progress/follow up.

vi Extended Opportunities Programs and Services (EOPS): a government-funded program established to provide special assistance to educationally and financially disadvantaged students.

vii Aid to Families with Dependent Children (AFDC): a federal program administered by the United States Department of Health and Human Services that provided financial assistance to children whose families had low or no income.

viii Cooperative Agencies Resources for Education (CARE): an additional service to Extended

Opportunities Programs and Services for single parents on AFDC with children under the age of six.

[ix] A re-entry center provides resources for the returning adult student seeking information about educational goals and career options. A re-entry student by definition is generally more than 24 years old or married with children and starting college for the first time or returning to college after a gap of a year or more.

[x] A Learning Center generally provides academic support programs and services, such as tutoring, supplemental instruction, study skills workshops and labs for learning and improving English.

[xi] An accelerated educational program is designed for working adults who wish to pursue undergraduate or graduate study, particularly meeting their needs with regard to scheduling and location of classes.

[xii] Some employers or companies contract with an outplacement firm to help one or more employees who leave the company transition out and into a new work or school situation. Their services may consist of helping with resume writing, interviewing, and other job search skills.

[xiii] Compartmentalization is an unconscious psychological defense mechanism used to avoid excessive mental stress and anxiety caused by having conflicting emotions within oneself.

[xiv] Scripture and/or notes quoted by permission. Quotations designated (NET) are from the NET Bible® copyright ©1996-2006 by Biblical Studies Press, L.L.C. All rights reserved.

www.ingramcontent.com/pod-product-compliance
Lightning Source LLC
Chambersburg PA
CBHW071839020426
42331CB00007B/1788